# *Brush Strokes*

By

*Ferris E. Jones*

# Contents

# A Solemn Forest

With chronic passion
I've dreamed of this solemn forest.
To stand and declare my motive;
To complete this deed.

Take me, my sins are worthy,
Sit me at the table.
Leave the little one to run gloriously
With memories of unwitting love.

There will be no dissent,
No time to repent.
No time to frown
I will witness his life,
I can look down.

# Baby Steps

In the drooling shade
Of the prosperous sun
The clouds masquerade
And the children run.

All things are divine
Under the tiny feet
Feelings will resign
The joy now complete.

# Social Media

Shall I welcome this affair,
With its fate and prepare?
Or become its next heir,
Fully willing to impair?

Witness to the death of friends,
The honor it descends?
Watch as last breath ascends,
Remember me when it ends?

# Grief

When lying in sufferance each night,
Remembering the days bright light.
At a heater vent calmly praying,
Above me it remains obeying.
While I toss out the day's events,
Inquire for peace without a doubt.
My loss to a portal I shout,
And each day I will wake without.
Small condolence will I receive,
Memories past, I will perceive.
Not sure of stories to believe,
In dreams fair, I solemnly grieve.

# Divorce

I can see her eyes so forlorn
With thoughts of gallant revenge,
The Gods are preparing to mourn.

The hedges manicured so pure
Like viewing her frame by frame,
When a marriage cannot endure.

Flowers flounce in the wind, passing
Free the car panics to leave,
The children's tears are harassing.

# Sunday

An unholy Sunday
Begins with the sacrament of wine.
The summoning of one's fancy
To watch the days first shine.

Oh, what a spirit it does bring
To the anointed pleasure.
The day's verse cries to behold
A soon to be written treasure.

# Shotgun

Her soul with wings secure
Shouts memories of light.
So fine, joy will endure
This life so simply bright.

Past in a star folding
The triumph in a dream lost.
So fine, the seat holding
Loves tremendous cost.

# Off-ramp

If I were more aware of the reason,
For standing still in this cold season.
The trepidation and lack of pity;
Would not require a vote by committee,
But a gesture fond of this new city.
I would read the sign and show some trust
On the new road ahead, that spits unjust.

# A Beautimous Slush Puppy

To know the number of rose buds she gathers
To wake up each day and know her love matters
To witness the blush of the beauty that gleams
To soundly sleep in a world of dreams.

Is to toast to a world that she deserves
Is to crawl the pathway that only serves
Is wine so delicate it must be free
Is a life with her that must always be?

# The Cuba Road Ghost

Lingering, human form
The White Cemetery shivers;
Hazy with light they swarm,
Teen scares their task delivers.

Age, best to remember
The drifting and gliding at last;
Memories of ember,
Rest peacefully in the past.

# The Solemn Promise of Art

The solemn promise of art,
To spill out the singing birds.
Rip out the one mighty heart,
And drain the body of words.

# Turning on a Hose

It's as a musician
Who can't read music.
I don't memorize the
Work of great masters,
Have a favorite Poet,
I haven't ambition.

I write what I see,
The sounds that I hear.
Words come out of the air,
From stimuli in place.
I just arrange them,
That's what makes me be.

# A Free Man

Here as a man I stand,
Pointing upward at the rules.
I will not live my life,
As those orderly walking fools.

Trust not money changers,
No morality flows within.
I break all norms daily,
Sleep peacefully with the dangers.

# Singing She Was

Singing she was
Each step of her walk,
Fell as if she could talk.

A toy was she
The Chrysanthemum,
For all the winds to strum.

The memory
Of a lion's old soul,
Forever to console.

# Love Undisturbed

Love undisturbed can't resist
The force from within,
We all enlist.

It's ripened wreath so restrained
Brings years calming peace,
A goal attained.

The bonds that adorn the light
Gathers strength in time,
To rest each night.

# Life's Trail of Grandeur

Life shines in its grandeur,
With dust hiding some cracks.
Allowing time to rest its gleam,
Leaving memories in its tracks.

Behold its fearless wonder,
The trail it leaves for you.
Its path is your freedom,
Don't waste it being a shrew.

# Yeah - Just the Wine

She stands each moon
Waiting with smiles.
They all start equal in the afternoon.

The disparity of the musing
Dragging through the moments.
Leave a few for her choosing.

# Homeless Voodoo Priestess

Oh, servant of the spirits,
what a profile you cut.
Please take this umbrella,
to shield you from the smut.

You say you cannot take it;
bad luck for a street person.
It can shield you my dear,
for that I am certain.

Then take this hot coffee,
bring my life some change.
Allow me to understand,
no want for this exchange.

# The Flash

I've seen the flash,
the being of youth.
Dreaming and dreaming,
of being a star.

Drugs, from one stop,
to the other. The clothes.
Leather boots, gold and gestures.
Sex, the running together of days.

# Words

Words, sometimes tragic;
spoken in haste.
Can decide your future;
cries of what you embraced.

# The Point

We pray each day,
endurance shows.
The gifts of life
we won't disclose.

What is left now,
for those to hold.
Depends on us,
the world is cold.

# Election

Shattered
Splattered
The bombs begin
To Blow.

Evolution
Revolution
The time has
Come to show.

# Grandson

Look at that old bench
there, by the tree.
Your grandmother said yes,
which made me, and thee.

# A Chicago Apartment

The tepid city lights,
hold tales of splendor.
Grateful for the knowledge
they will not surrender.

Castaway's stare out with thunder,
pacing along with time.
Not asking for the answers,
that is their crime.

# A Short Walk

The joy of not being confined to wander scared
Like the lost child who learns to forget home
In the pleasantness of the dry grass and garbage
Spread out like a message of fate declared.
Sits on the soul of an old man when the wind
Blows the plastic bag across the brown weeds
When a simple walk of no intention finds him so
Sure, the past is clear, and he has not sinned.

# Snoqualmie Falls

The drive, the sun and the spring air,
Deep with its noon breath rests quietly
As real beauty, undenied and fair.
Falls with the rationality
By participating with laws,
Ending in functionality.
Superb with its new collection
Of calm, voiceless sapphire pools,
Lending truth to God's perfection.

# The Playground

I walked to the implicated courtyard,
And witnessed what was planted;
The foundation was still the same,
A place I had taken for granted.

This was the cradle of all time,
The location where thought derived;
A haunting picture of thorns,
The yard where my innocence died.

# A Summer Night

Yeah, I was pissed,
The glowing moon, fed;
Nothing but dreams,
Of the last one kissed.

The wind didn't blow,
Or smell of new night,
It just threw back,
The moon's silent light.

Tossed back a shot,
To get past my thoughts;
Still on the porch,
Feeling, what was brought.

# Teenager

Not all that long ago,
I was him; and he was
Alone without family norms,
Never to be one who conforms.

No thought for convention.
No faith in ascension.

A boy without a home,
I was him; and he was
Alone without any form,
Or knowledge of how transform.

No thought of what he needs.
No faith in how he pleads.

# Time in the Ground

I stood among my many years
And read the past days of others.
The grass was even with each step
And the surroundings well maintained.
I wondered if they were happy
And if time would find us all peace.
It's where we spend most of our time
And should be comfortable at least.

# Sins of your Youth

I've been angry at the world,
Contemplating its quick demise.
I've watched the foe of sunrise
And in it held the days disguise.
I've done things, stories are told,
Still to this old wonderful day.
I watch the children dream and play,
Aware someday; I will pay.

# The Gold Fish

Time did not ravish my failure
To defend your honor my sister.
I stood in fear,
When I should have fallen.
The beating I took from years
Still paints in my tears,
Our fathers swarm of memory,
And a walk home from the carnival.
The joy you held in your hand
Was taken from you by others.
The fish that lay dying,
Has now become your brothers.

# Night Terrors

In each, lives the thought,
Of the nights tremendous wrought.
Scream with the walking rain
The time, sleep, it will detain.
Holds up the mind with dreams,
Without comfort so it seems.
A parent's hug redeems,
But they're gone and it sees.

# Thinking

In the midst of this falling hour,
I sit and ponder God's tower.
With feeble attempts, I witness,
My soul's unique unfitness.
Neglected burning's I seek,
Maybe, I can gain a peek.

# Once Upon a Mattress

Here, as a fan, I sit,
The theater is authentic,
Consciousness is surprising
While the scene is still rising.
The warm spring laughter is mine,
The blushing voices are time.
It reminds me of old ways,
Bruka, the good old days.

# Perception

Welcome,
Become the unseen existence
My friend; my beautiful habit.
Embrace the moments and find your way
The nights undiminished-
For you my glowing attribute.

Join the vast divinity of bewildered eyes
And cry your tears with barbed conquering
Feel the thunder of murmured tongues-
Then pick the reality that keeps you high.

Choose the ancient way - the smoking spirit.
To walk the barefoot path of a continuous forest.
Enter the doors without hurried words,
Steal its features of blissful whispers.

It's here my friend: my beautiful habit.
Where oblivion has come to die
And the appearance of the moon
Can change a man's merit.

Join me - stay with me.
Forever we can be together.
Among the many unexpected visions
We can find our way,
A brilliance in
In a particular world.

# The Virgin

Do we know if virgins are happy
So fair in their character?
Do they blush with wicked words?

Have we all forgotten they are heavenly stars
To be discovered?
Their mysteries have knowledge.
Their dreams are real.

From the farthest dawning of undiscovered lands
They travel with time and hope,
Testing - celebrating old symbols
And the Gods that accompany them.

Have we forgotten the ancient copulations
That created our temples?

Hope sprang from the sea to grant us the choice.
Will we live as unbodied obscene creatures
Or will we accept the journey put forth?
The one we know will end in death.

A virgin cannot conceal their emptiness,
Nor should they claim their passions are no more.

There is art in their walk
An Innocence passes from the window from which they watch
All of those weary in the indecision and thought
Of a melancholy soul.

We all must do the dance
The dance of invisible hunger
The eternal darkness
The rain in which we all get wet,

We assemble our lives with mortal strain
Which gives us the right
To pass whole
No matter the choices that are made,

# The Desert

I have crawled to the desert
Watered the sagebrush with mushrooms.
Sullen in my decision - I have spoken
With the four winds
And received my apparition.

The nameless rest on breasts of eloquent distortion
And the calls for darkness never end.

Trees will die from a lack of judgment.
Babies will be born without sight.
Remorse will not be taught in school,
While the Petroglyph's sit in passive despair.

# To Know Me

One might think to have known me.
Yet never translated my purpose.
Nor asked about the time of deaths mishap.
It's in black and white; the struggles
In identifying the real and unreal.

It just takes a short minute to complete
The small purchase of a man's soul.
Then open it up and peer into it.
It's hidden there in plain sight,
The days of darkness; the days of light.

# Don't Wait

The glory of lingering light
Cannot kill the thirst
For past apologies.

They have not departed
But just float as dust
In the eclipsing mirror of time.

Only when fragments of the end
Stare back at you
Will the clock chime.

# The Rise and Fall of Kingdoms

We can be touched by fire,
Dance with Coca Cola thoughts-
Fall between conflicts.

Witness nations born naked,
Others crumbling under dictatorship-
Live in a time of peace.

Hope for better days,
Spend jubilant seconds with birth-
Be godlike when events are historic.

It's where we fall,
That is our greatest gift-
It's been given to us all.

# Don't Wait

The glory of lingering light
Cannot kill the thirst
For past apologies.

They have not departed
But just float as dust
In the eclipsing mirror.

Only when fragments of the end
Stare back at you
Will the clock chime.

# Waves - Field of Dreams

Pilgrims of wrath they drench unconditionally.
I admire the consistency of the wave's immortality.
Faithful to the end they pound and consume.
Blessed the path they intend to entomb.
Like acid winds of vision, they appear.
The knowledge of savior is contained in its fear.
Once you understand why the enemy is there.
You can contemplate and compare.
The pain you feel is never as it seems.
The waves can carry you to your own field of dreams.

# Everyday

Everyday,
Without fail,
I hear from the dead,

Nobody knows that.

They have all turned over.

Can't believe what they see,
Can't believe what has happened to their world,
Their country!!

They ask,
How can a man who once wanted to be part of a revolution,
A man who felt the SLA and IRA had a place in this world
Watch and do nothing?

How can we all - let shame ponder in the eyes of our children?
Why would we expect heaven to be glorious?
If we are not willing die for something on earth?

Without the sight of the departed- what do we live for?
Our deeds must be many and virtuous or we pass without eyes.
We are but the dead on this earth.

We must rise and defend our lives here, NOW
If not,
We will have no eternal peace.
Be remembered by none.

We will stare downward in anguish for eternity
And cry for the lost opportunity of our children.

# Independence Day

It's the day of our Independence.

Where are the super hero's?

The men - the women - who will stand against tyranny?

Those who will take barbaric forms and silence hypocrisy
While heaven's rain falls.

We need conquerors who breath winged azure
To descend upon the villainous heard.

Stake claim to freedom.
Play songs without gunfire.

Walk the fiercest road and
Claim its steps for America.

We will not give back that which was earned.

You cannot steal what is not yours.

We will join together in the costume of an army if needed
And defeat our enemies.

# Death of a Rock Star

Not sure how he passed away,
Just a nudge in one's sleep.
Looked at me but could not stay,
It's time he declared to weep.

So, I woke and wiped the tears,
Witnessed the others convene.
Slowly a band mate appears,
Pulls him up from the ravine.

# Workaholic

Who rests in the haggard plot,
With pathetic crackling flowers?
Buried, loitering, too young to rot.
Consequence; no regard for hours.

Decades lost fill this tomb,
The joy only for others care.
Forgotten his deeds did not bloom.
His short relentless life rests where?

# Maybe

He lives without friends,
nor angel's heaven sent.
Someone, come find him,
to stop his hearts lament.

Walk with him this day.
bring with you some hope.
Then maybe, just maybe,
he may decide to stay.

# Wandering Thoughts

On my left side
I lay with thoughts,
of words dancing,
with three winks.

On my right side,
I lay with thoughts,
of feelings banging,
with three knocks.

Face down-head turned,
I lay with thoughts,
telling my son,
it's hereditary.

# Home

In the rows of homes,
with drunkard's heart.
Built with dreams,
that soon depart.

A man who walks tall,
can learn from this fall.

He sees how lives are led,
feels the pain that's fed.
Learns the string of song,
prays the days are strong.

His children will captain,
the dreams that happen.

# Bad Day

They always start with a phone call,
text, or maybe an email.
Pulling in 7-11, to pick up some *O'Doul's.*
Never mind, its *Coors Light,* my
sister has just died. Found on the kitchen
floor. After a little bit of drinking. Two days later,
without any sleep. Our father has a stroke, falls.
His nose is broken. It's *Super Bowl Sunday,* my
team is playing. They lose. Look ridiculous.
Vodka and *Diet Pepsi* for a year.
Pills are always cheap. It's sleep that you pay for.

# A Tapho Heart

The lights come
up: Stage right-
rows of polished granite
list names, dates.
They are not
in sequence.
A middle-aged man
kneels, cries.
Careful not to stand
for she is not there.
But she did
leave her mark.


# In Heaven

In Heaven
the tongue is pure,
words pass through
grieved souls
to build bridges
of resistance;
throwing back
tyranny.

# Sands of Time

Till the thought
of love, becomes
a meditating
covenant. Mankind
will be told
by a master,
when the sands
of time
will submit.


# Death Like Wine

Death like wine
breathes,
anticipates.
A moment is an
outstretched hand
welcoming,
a vibrant
aftertaste.

# The Man Called Coach

With a slap of the leather,
crack of the bat, and the
score board lights cheering
the home team.
The memories of a young boy;
have become the nightmare of an old man.

How young boy wanted to see the Dodgers play!
How the tears fell when washing
his uniform in the bathtub!
He knew he was the only one not going,
and his drunken father would never know.
But for one night and one night only
a man would take his father's place, and the
young boy would go to his first baseball game.

While the Red Stocking's uniform hung on
the shower curtains. The young boy's
mind thought back to how he explained to coach
he couldn't find his father,
and he had no money for the game.
But that's ok; he would be at their game tomorrow
because he would just ride his bike.
He had learned early on that day dreaming helped
stop the hunger pains, and all he had was TV.

Then a knock at the door, and standing there
was the man he called coach. "Let's go", he said.
Soon the wet uniform carried no cause or thought,

for he was looking at his daydreams coming true,
and again, it's something his father never knew.
This would be the greatest night of his life;
a Dodger dog and soda the greatest meal
of his life. For one night a coach had taken the place
of his drunken father, and he was never happier.

# For Just One Day

He walks unbearable,
with aimless meander
toward a ritual.
To pray a soul,
for just a day
can claim the realm,
come out,
and play.

Visit just once the
formal province.
Speak the funny influence
that followers remember.
Let them hear the word,
and retain those joys.
Reimburse yourself like
only you deserve.

# A War for Oil

To pillage has
no honor. It denies
great men, what
is due. One
could lose a son.
Sons could lose
a brother. A
Daughter in law
could lose a
husband. A little
boy could lose
a father. And this
is but one family.
Of many.

# Trailer Park Art

Just an average Saturday night,
Staring at the walls.
Drunk off my ass,
When an idea came forth.
If he becomes a famous artist,
Then I became a famous poet.
This could really be worth something.

So, I took out my 9 mm,
Aimed it at the face on the wall.
Fired a shot on target,
A collaboration between artists.

The bullet hit its mark,
Passing through the paintings eye.
Passing through the living room wall.
Passing through the bedroom wall.
Passing through the bathroom wall,
Coming to rest,
On the shattered toilet,
That never crossed my mind.

Sunday morning appears.
Going from store to store.
Could not find a replacement,
In such a quiet place.
I spent the rest of the day in the bar,
Obviously, because they had a toilet.

# Battle

My muse, happy as you wander,
Witness with the fountains,
About life, we ponder.

The deluge, of serpents dancing,
War against you rages,
Evil, and the ages.

From below, we thank your vision,
Safe arms we feel complete,
With you, life is so sweet.

# Money in His Wallet

With quiet little fingers
The boy pulls a knife,
As a thought lingers.

No food in the house
He steps without fear,
Sees who brought him here.

Passed out on the couch
The drunkard snores,
Lunch in his back pouch.

He cuts to get cash
He will never know,
Be sure and go slow.

With gaze, he wakes
Eyes see death in mind,
The child he shakes.

"You better kill me",
Replied the drunken fool.
Hungry and now school.

# Reunion

Those unremembered prophecies
Of friends from the past.
The faces and names still crying
The reasons still last.

Boundless gleams appear with moments
Of silence and dreams.
The battle to remember the sins
Feels forever screams.

Sorry I can't seem to place you
It's gone inside me.
Hiding from those captive waters
I must pay my fee.

# Conflict

Don't reject the fear
of conflict.
Covet it like a
sunny day;
hope it continues,
let it stay.
Know you're alive;
world will strive.
You will live - and thrive.

# A Letter

Funny, seeing a letter.
Brings a belief,
in the old ways,
while senses spill
the reading light,
of heaven.

# A Funeral in the Rain

The rain staggered the tress
and melted the ground with leaves.
Simplifying this day's struggle
for which tomorrow will double.

No rites heard handed down
and no prayer to stop the sound.
This pain of decision
forever in precision.

# Fall Television

The cost
The frost

The model
The bottle

Springs and sings
Football brings.

# Hell

they piled the bodies
for convenience,
then dug pits

they befriended the death
laughed at time,
Satan permits.

# Ashes in Nevada

I will come for you,
the dreams will know again,
the vast green scenery.

I will come for you,
no judge of gold sitting,
just hands to hold the past.

I will come for you,
to carry you home quiet,
to rest in peace at last.

# Long Drive

In a surrounding of comfort
in cellophane pulled
from a pack of Marlboro reds,
cross tops pass across the bar.
It's a long drive to Chicago,
a straight thirty-six hours. A
new cassette and he's set.
Turns to say goodbye,
the twin hookers' wave,
smiling at what the
bartender just gave.

# Today

The newborn seed is what we need
To claim our place
At the table first,
With an idea of life embraced.

In moment's we recall the fall
Leads to a day
Finding the time,
That rules now cannot betray.

# The Politics of Chaucer

Run from hate and embrace the new;
Scamper the wind to live with all;
Don't hide the thoughts we all know stew;
Embarrassment for it is small;
Change the pattern before you fall;
Find the mind to care of beauty,
Be one with us, it's your duty.

# My Bride

This is what I assure when our hands meet,
the sufferance of my soul can feel it deplete.

The certainty of love hovers as we patiently lay,
devours from the goddess the words we will say.

Heaven speaks of you as suns first start,
and stars hold my love, until death do us part.


# 2016 –

The newest transformation denies
And brings with it nothing but fear
It sits with a tongue of lies,
While Democracy sips its smear.

Its grandeur he aims to change
And destroy our traditions
With it a man of derange,
Steals our children's ambitions.

# Life's Melodies

What nature gives or takes
at birth, is almost of no worry.
It's what you took, from all
the misguided steps,
that lets you sleep.

Do not let the affluent struggles
bind your reason, throw each
away like a wishful penny. Then watch
as we all do; it's slow turn
until it hits the bottom.

# Precious Thought

A bard tossed of precious thought,
Awakes each night, eyes distraught.
To feel the words precise and clear,
The days outset he must not fear.
With time and wit, he will not lie,
True penned musings cannot die.

# All Children

Measured by a moment
Of outstanding kissing's,
Better than all day spent,
On all the small missing's.

A nascent child clamors
With each delightful time,
Life fruitful completes,
The clock begins to chime.

# The Span

And as she was whisked away
people are walking the streets,
unaware of loss present,
while this day completes.

The glory that awaits her
beginning from the birth,
passes the bystanders pace,
then begins a new earth.

# U-Haul

Up the confident coast to live the sea,
And a volcano stares fatherhood:
And on this road a future pardoned stood,
And a life can witness all it could be.

# The Ministry

Alone in the country side
Seeking purpose,
They find allegiance
And disdain for their brother.

Left alone without thought,
Without windows,
Nothing of themselves is real
And they will let go of each other.

# A Long Walk with Flowers

The thorn points at
sober beauty,
waiting
for the
hard moment
to show you
it's life.

# Wake up

The sky begins to open its eye,
efficient and delicious;
at night it says goodbye.

Ornate reminiscent of true fate,
sufficient and ambitious;
morning never late.

# Dreams

No,
it's not real.
Just a play
that keeps
acting in
my head.
I think,
I'll ask
it to stay.

# To Those Who Break at Dawn

Much of what the sun does
Gives light to terrible things.
Much of what the sun loves
Brings purpose to our dreams.

An open path for you
To choose the day's intention.
Determine what is past due
Give it the attention.

# You Don't Need Money to be Yourself

They have found the scenes
To strut magnificent spheres.
And yet they have no means
Then sadly it all disappears.

# Newspeak

Where does your ego rest
On a putrid sheet of lies?
Knowing of the worlds detest
The truth you simply disguise.

Conceit will topple down walls
Of all the righteous fake kings.
It's your presence that appalls
And a sentence the bird sings.

# Untalented Visionary

The inner reality
may be slowly perceived.
Words are not always born,
sounds are to be believed.
The echoes of a loss,
thunderclaps the bereaved.

# Rule of the People

We stand fair and free
Citizens unheeding
To the uncontrolled
Serpents biblical plea.

Protect regardless
Without color or fame
Fight the shameful
Vote out those who oppress.

Rule of law system
For all to be included
The vile Dictator
We will struggle to condemn.

# The Salesman

Much time I've spent on this road,
Searching in my dreams of peace seen.
Hoping that God would intervene,
To translate with faith that's bestowed.
With mysteries help to decode.

Strangers confuse the city's roar,
With the endless dribble of the skies.
It's in the small things that hope lies,
Slowly walking to heaven's door.
The signs set forth you can't ignore.

# What if God

What if God
played over and over
with a hundred-dollar bill?
Making it appear out of reach,
maybe the ink runs.
Floating it upwards as
a song continues to play.
With ears ringing
and people around
in an almost circle
it floats again.
Then the morning paper;
Capricorns can
speak to the divine,
get closer to God,
see him, feel him,
talk directly to him,
and get answers from him.
If they follow the
money trail.

# Gates

If the gates of heaven were opened
to all for just one day.
Who would be seen in a glow
without a flame?
Would Martin Luther King be
seated next to Thomas Jefferson
while a Confederate flag hangs
high waving?

And if the gates of hell were opened
to all for just one day.
Who would be seen in the
pit of fire without a light?
Would Adolph Hitler be
seated next to Nostradamus
while his staff stands stiff
in the water?

# The News

On what day will a
mother's eye tear
to walk
the path of dread,
the bloody thorns
pushed on and around
the head of the unbeliever?

When will a distance
be shown
cracking, laughing,
burning with the sun
destruction of greenery
and a dog unheard?

# You #1

I'm the man who places
that small curtain
above your window.
The one who obscures
your vision,
only in part.
I can stop the sun
from coming
upon your face.
Without ever asking you
for anything.
I'm the one you wish
to kick,
when the blanket
covers your feet,
and the one
you seek to hold
when the snow
is falling deep.

# Evolution

What evolution has brought us here?
Where winged creatures fly so fiercely
with deliberate species calculation.
What age has dissolved the upward pleasure?
To burrow and hoard amongst the
very vastness of fossils, clinging
to the dirt from which it crawled.
Is it to be the wings?
Unfortunate begetting of brethren with
claws that must fight, always
for survival emerging from the caves

# Word

The eclipse was
last night.
But its echo
still lingers.
Over the trees
the clouds paint
like morning rain.
A speck of blue brings
drops to the heart
and pain
upon a word,
so hard it
is to be spoken
everyday.

# Smooth

The smooth polished hardness
sits quietly in a child's hand
cascading vast crevices.

The beauty withstood the outspoken
motive of energy leading to its
birth between land and sea.

Placed just from a time
as a dust to blow back
to its home
between land and sea.

# Noah's Ark

Many eyes witnessed
the loading of the ark.
Couples or pairs
all creatures were placed,
next to those who had
never seen such wonders.
A black man and woman
lay together with the Jew
who cried when the King
sat with his mistress
and the cat,
as the toad sleeps.

# The Girl in White

No mark has secured this
bridge rarely traveled.
The shortness of white
portrays the years as
painted with trouble.

It disturbs a beginning,
the adolescent atrocities
in disguise,
a foreboding
detail accessed,
spindling of thoughts
born inside of depths.

# John the English

The modern papacy was not
defined by ancient scripture,
but re-written as a new
type of book in twelve languages.
It contains the views of
women like John the English
giving birth to a child.
Always uncovering a lie,
not being that which God
has put forth.
Takes a piece away
from the form
of belief.

# A Coffee Can in the Attic

It's folded over by machines
holding the DNA of mankind.
With blood, objects are placed inside
delicately, hiding it for a time.

Shells sound the children's walk
playing wet with earth clinging.
A distant memory presses
against the heads of the forgotten.

A skull, dead like Nevada cattle,
a Texas tie gets placed inside
to be gone until life gets
remodeled or
children rule the present.

# Naked

The pure naked coin
was not enough to stop the
crucifixion of our son.
The balance of money and power
would never be passed over,
from that moment forward.
Those who are to work
for that band of gold displayed
on the sleeve of indulgence,
go home to have supper only
when the phone stops ringing.

# College

The leaves are what are remembered,
laughing in its gathering of corners.
The sun sleeps its short day
and the dread of pain sets a lovely table
for the one who stays behind.

The dreams are held by writing in moods
to the music of long phone calls.
Praising them each night to sleep,
in the silence of what was once
a necklace of laughter.

The thoughts are believed to be
centered on a friend's disappointment.
Seeing it as a road trip,
the real stories of a life,
and an attempt to be a real boy.

# War of 1812

The picture of the first King
must be broken.

God has set forth a schedule,
as the President paints
the countryside.
For if the fires burn
longer than two suns can turn,
the winds shall bring
the tears of God
and the tornado shall put out
the fire of the British.

# She's Late Again

She's late again,
reruns are raging
the gangster flick is reaching its climax
and thoughts are jumping rope.

She's late again,
the demons
come back
to draw another crooked line
next to the other.

The past inefficiencies bewilder
the passing of time
in years
meaning experience is only
Gods will for you.

# The Track They Walk

They claim to be good mothers,
but the track they walk
is laid out on their arms,
like the mark of the beast.
Prominent and boastful
they're homeless.
Tattooed are the numbers
of the thief,
liar,
and the whore.
They have done deeds
which kings in tents
resting in the desert
beneath the wondrous star
have spoken against and
words have been passed
on for two thousand years.

# Fire

Spit at me
with hells fire you
blasphemer and fornicator
you bitch.
Declare yourself unto thee,
betrayed but loved
the people wait for you
to witness the growing
because the time has come,
carbon is here,
you must strike.

# Exorcism

The thoughts transfer
in tongues,
lips are chapped
with pure
spring water.
The Pope's dream team
not available
at this time.
There are places for the poor
to pray
and state their name.
The king's horses will be
tied up out front
the king's men
will come
when Satan
has taunted them.

# Monkey Information

It's as if one monkey
whispered to another
down, down the row
they go.
Changing direction until
a decision is made.
Down, down fall the bodies
from the interpretation.
A species who can't remember
where it came from
brings death to
its own clan.

# The Code

We see the cross
chastise our body
and feel the temptation
of sacrifice
each living second
the church cries.
The blood of Christ
is taken whole
with the body
from his soul.
Hoping and praying
that the sins
of creators have not
damned us to drown
in the wine for which
we create our children.

# The Hitchhiker

It's dark and I'm tired,
dazed with flickering lights.
I see the flowing robe
in the middle of the road.
With a thumb out for a ride,
slow to see the car pull over.
My sister who has been gone
picks up the robe and
goes the other way.
With hands he gives direction,
she pays no attention, and
takes him far away. That is
why the black cat which ran into
the street, turned around with fear
when hit by the light.

# Books

In a sleep
hurt by the actions of self,
the devil is a ball and chain
showing himself within
the blood of Christ.
Ingested with certainty
is a death wish.

But then a light
comes as forgiveness,
and the son speaks though tears,
and the crying child
allows peace to continue
with a joy
and a fondness for books.

# Iran

Please don't take my little boy,
his hands have never seen powder.
Rubber bands at his brother,
and laughter was war.
His face speckled like the dunes,
faithful like the desert wonderers.
He would be too good at it,
or die trying.
His heritage would not let
him give or surrender.
For he took the land,
for which he breaths.
Please do not take my little boy,
because if asked he would go.

# Grail

I am a ghost
lying witness
to my stumbling.
Befallen, murdered
by the guns
of my own nature.
I have control
and see others
as facts that dwindle
the guards of God,
light chose a foe
the holder of the Grail.
I declare,
I will return
like another
five hundred
years from now.

# Junk Yard

There is life in there
underneath the mangled,
torn, and shredded carcasses
deposited one on top the other.
Forensic scientists would have a day
in the field overgrown
under-nourished with a
collection of debris
tossed away in typical
fashion of Capitalism.
What crimes are buried?
Gone unreported, sitting
waiting to be uncovered
wanting peace to be bought.
For decades it sits
until the same system
which put it there
finds more money
in planting seeds
and families there.

# Place

The drinks are served
the movie is
The Wizard of Oz.
Don't look for
the witch outside.
The door is down
they feel God's will
be done.
Who shall prevail?
The plane is
the object, and
with hands
it shall crash.
Who will go
to what place?

# Strings

By the strings we
are the Roman Empire.
Paying for the leaders
concubines dressed
in nowhere.
Consumers paying
for music
written
by the hand
of a man
proclaimed by birth
to follow history
and be dads
little man standing
where Jesus
walked
asking for help.

# Regrets

I've always loved your
words of
drunken slumber.
You turn life open
to the outside.
With leaves falling
from the trees.
Falling, branches
snapped and broken,
wanting to be back.
Spring is a long way,
and it always
brings regret.

# The Bible

The Bible sits
unread
wondering for
a better understanding
of children
who will read it.
Read it,
ask the questions.
Who will be there?
Wait and see
the regret will show you
the time you have
to find the answer.

# Change

Some thinkers know it's wise
to pay attention to the
opinions and ideas of those
who came before, Some of these
views could be extreme but
are no less valid.  Maybe
the world and all things in
at are in constant change.
Maybe nothing remains the same.
But in the world of Parmenides
nothing ever changes. Permanence
reigns supreme.  Our world is only
perceived by the senses.  So, who
really hears what?

# Creation

In a land untouched by
humans, a pure work of God or
nature – seeds spring with trees,
as white sands shift about.
Quakes open cones, form the
land.  Birth and death are created.
A great work of art.
Not just as man, is
artificial or as he interprets
that which is around him.
But man can only create
man – and not the land.

# House of Windsor

What was the house of Windsor
before they decided not to hold
anything with German arms?  Why
would Landon be the center
of new world order views?  The
birth of the two sons will carry
with it the new views.  With the
mother dead – no one can contest
the superiority.  Nor speak against
a world with one ruler.  Hand
picked by families, whom by their
deeds should have been wiped
out of existence – centuries before.

# Kings

Kings, presidents, and princes
stand forth and pledge their
belief that God commands
over man is false.  That all
the biblical concepts
need be renounced
and all people need to
embrace the stewardship
that they were
born into – and watch
them obey because the
enlightened minds will be
working as groups to
insure their daily feeding.

# Israel

Israel's birth of Jesus ultimately
leads to the secret
plans of the order.  He
who controls this land
controls the oil fields,
and when Armageddon comes
it will start in Jerusalem,
for it is the home of the
three great religions.  The
pagan philosophy will be
working towards a one-world
government, in an attempt
to undermine all political and
religious order.  So, goes all
Christian morals and
democratic values.

# The Leader

Saddam had to be hung
for rebuilding the great city
to pay honor to Satan.
The rituals and festivals paid
Tribute to the pagan Gods –
while the anti-Christ is coming.
Fifty attempts before
all have failed because
his soul was protected
by Satan.

# Population

Black nobility, I say
is only obedient to their own
agenda.  The complete control
of every human on earth.
The feudal system as it once
Was is back and only
The souls needed to complete
the hereditary leader's tasks,
will remain.  The rest will die
due to restrictions placed
on population.  Hitler's
crematoriums burn without fire.
The middle class has been killed
and you rule, serve, or die.

# The Valley

Bring down your fucking warriors,
or lord lets bestir the valley.
Let Joel proclaim the nations
swords, and I will sit in
judgment of these lords. Put
a sickle for harvest or drink
the wine.  But the lord will
still destroy the armies of hate
and once this peace has been
confirmed, the Chinese with
their secret road to Tibet will
again threaten.

# One Mistake

Let's all read revelations so
we can see how the end of days
will come. The history channel show
is more likely to be accurate.  It
speaks not of a Fuhrer or anti-Christ.
But something we most likely brought
upon ourselves destroyer to blame,
or regal lion who sits on the
throne of death, counting souls
as he laughs at God. But someone is
just waiting for a mistake -
this will let him reign.

# The Killer

Jesus has been predicted to come
in thousands of prophecies. Those who
claim to be the seers say
end of days is here. When
will I see him? When is faith enough?
The bible reads the second beast
is a Jew. Jesus was a Jew. No
matter what Christians believe. They
say he has magic – just as Jesus
did. If the movie is correct and
history has shown us anything,
it's that you can kill anybody.
The false prophet and our so-
called dictator must die. The
man, who does it will be put
to death. Nobody but God
will ever know of his great deed.

# Electronically

People now – since the computer
Age, are numbered from birth to
death. The government, will not
allow a human being not to
have a number. All transactions
must be done electronically.
Since the false prophet
will glorify this new form.
Death must come to him,
must come to the new
dictator and the real-world war
needs to be led by one of us.
Not Satan or the false prophet.
But us, whom we
must see our own heads roll.

# God in the Desert

Satan will send a piece of shit
who will have a fantastic power?
placed upon him. He will be given
a throne for which he will sit
and spit his will to all nations.
No miracles just tricks for
which the weak and unsure will
believe. The Dragon will only have
the power over man that he allows
him to have. Society is ripe and weak;
for we are all over-weight video game
rapists who pray on the old ways.
We will deserve this temptation if,
we continue to place our guards
with the television companies. Who
don't have the balls to resist;
God in the desert.

# Gary S.

It took a decade
of study
to receive
the discipline necessary
to must cleanse the
mind of all
the clutter coming
from the teachings
around us. We have
to find the separation
of matter and spirit.
Climb to the mountain
top, here we can write
free of the newly
found loneliness.

# Accuracy

The world could not have
order or arrangement without some
sort of thought. This must be
similar to mans. If we could not see
or think about order. It would not
be there. It's like one giant working
part with many little ones. There
are so many we can't conceive how
they are together. But through the
thought process we can
conclude there is some
sort of arrangement of these parts.
The accuracy itself
could not have been done by man,
it must have been done by
someone who thinks like man.

# Secular Times

For most rural Americans
industrialism became the terror.
They could not adjust to
the routines of the day. Many
became overwhelmed and found
peace in alcohol. This of course
outrageous to the conservatives.
Who consumed on a huge scale?
Times unlike today were secular
and everybody was expected
to hold certain disciplines. Oral and
anal became intensified by this
new so-called order and efficiency.

# Garden

The mother of mankind had
a dream conceived by Satan.
The lies he whispered convinced
her to go against the idea
she was more beautiful than all to come
before or after. She was the
companion to man, weaker morally
but obedient to her husband. As
she tends the garden, the dream
weakens her loyalty and she
leaves her man's side. Believing the
serpents lie she commits an
everlasting sin, forcing herself and
her husband to leave the
garden's paradise, hand in hand
with Michael as he explains they
will return.

# Economy

There is too much
civilization,
too much industry and means
of subsistence. What will be
done with all this commerce?
The bourgeoisie get no more
from this. They must create
disorder and fight for
what is theirs. They will never
compromise or share
the wealth.
They must conquer new markets
to prevent their own destruction.
By doing so, they bring into
existence those
who will carry out their deaths.

# There out There

It's the Democratic societies which
hold no esteem for meditation.
Since the turbulent years have passed
there appears no need for it.
Constant activities and addictions of
our minds can't find the time.

There is no time to contemplate our
thoughts or actions. We spend more
time pursuing false principles than
thinking that there are
some true ones out there. Passions
no longer decide our daily actions.

# The Future

We are all murderers, we killed
the holiest and most powerful king.
The blood can never wash off
and the ceremonies to bring him back
are but false presentations. We still
erect buildings in his honor.
Yet they are really just tombs.
Most people are not even aware
of his death. Every day they simply
go about their business. Not
realizing the foundation of society
on earth lies in ruins and will
someday crumble even further into despair.

# Not Given to Us

Man has the will to live
from taking his first breath. He
knows not at all if of any importance
it will serve. Living for man
is the same as it is for any
other animal. The reason is to live.
No deity has handed man a meaning
to live. That comes from within
each person. For if prominent enough
our meaning could surpass anything
that was given to us-including life.

# Hippies Created Hippies

The counter culture boys
and girls began rejecting
the virtues of the parents.
Masculinity, cleanliness, and
achievement was being confronted.
Polls showed the adults
as angry with
these dissident youth more
than the Viet-Nam war. This
pattern has shown
to be breaking down for
the last eighty years, and
parents still fail to realize
that the ideas
come from themselves.

# Greatness

Having a desire for knowledge
is one thing, the desire to use
it is another. Few minds have an
inexhaustible love for the truth.
One would need to tear apart
his soul and devote it. Give up
his own life to pursue the passions
and witness them come into being.
Hold the splendid objects that
come from it. Give it to society
and show them how great
mankind can be.

# Mother # 66

As a decade passed the
birth rate declined to below
four children. With the
creation of Mr. Lincoln it
declined even more. Ministries began
to preach and write - of Gods ways
for having and raising children. Less
children meant
more corruption, lack of
values and the more self-indulgent
people. It was declared
the Protestants
the responsibility
for all new nation's children
should fall upon the mother.

# Working Class

The bourgeoisie practice Capitalism
while the proletariat beg
until bodies give out.
The Lords want the
barbarians in the civilization;
it's still the will of a king
which rules. A Feudal society with
political sway and economic
power. Resting in the hands of
the few. The gigantic means
force work for the modern
working class.

# What Happened to the Old Days?

In the 1950's there seemed
to be a winner when a boy
meets a girl. The boys had to
persuade the girl he wanted to
be with her. The girl had to believe
him and show her interest.
First base, then second
base had to occur. The boy needed
to report back something, while the
girl needed to give up as little as
possible. In the end the girl was
successful for having a steady
boyfriend
and keeping her
virginity,
declared the winner.

# Wealth

For us as man
lies the natural impulse
to reach for thought
at the highest level.
To seek,
and live,
to love for truth.
science times can carry
itself away by the theories.

They feel nothing
but contempt for its practice,
and want the grandest
effort of our intellect to
lead to greater wealth.
Only the rich have any
time to seek gratification
to or for the mind.

# Worship

It is extremely difficult to
prove something exists. If doubt
has been cast. Worst is for the
individual who decides to take the
challenge. The difference lies not
in if God really exists. But if the
idea "God exists" is true or not.
What is meant by concept that an
old white-haired man sitting on
a throne somewhere is caring for us.
Why would he care for us? He is
thought of by man in many different
ways, he transcends anything with
regards to space and time. In order
to be worshiped he must be
conceived as omnipresent.

# Old Movies & Writing

Men still confused to this day
how their once traditional
domination of women has disappeared.
Roles changed, the divorce rate climbed,
women began to work. A mans
fear was even shown to the masses.
Women were always scheming. So, one
answer was to find a Doris Day.
The writing changed, women were
always tempting the heroes,
the stronger more
willful man would always save
himself from the seductress.

# Christmas

In America the family was
once displayed with vigor,
now it has been
reduced to
a mere money relation.
Santa Claus is simply
a teller machine,
who stands still - fat
with cash
waiting for someone to
write out their list,
then push his button.
He gives you the stamps
waits patiently for the person
with a dream to come by.
So at least he sees a smile,
in a camera.

# Lords Greatest Creation

He is the enemy, the
light-bearer and father of the
mass murderers
the stars of documentaries,
the personification of evil
and the creator of lies and
false ambition. His many men,
sin and death sit beside him
as sons of honor.
Fallen from the hand of the
universe
he plots against the
greatest creation.
He stands tall before man, but
small in the eyes of the Lord.

# Predisposed

Man has always been very eager
to pursue physical gratification.
Being dissatisfied and free allows
time to increase their fortune.
Their mind is predisposed to seek
the shortest route. They will diminish
the cost of whatever is necessary to
facilitate this pleasure they seek.
The greatest effort does not always
mean the greatest satisfaction. Man
must not confuse effort with results.

# 60's  # 4

Our cities began to deteriorate. Indians
were forced to survive on welfare. The
reservations were full forcing them
to enter the slums, with thousands
of black, and poor whites. What happened
to the Kennedy prophecy and Johnson's
agreement that all we needed was some
urban planning?
The ideas faded out
and the cities were never renewed,
inflation began to take hold. But
a man did land on the moon
scientists were kidnapped.

# Creator

The argument of all arguments
before man
was not to seek shelter
or obtain food. It was above them
in the night sky.
There exists nothing greater.
A creator needs to be
conceived.
nature
there cannot be anything greater
than what caused this.
By nature
thought
there must exist a creator.

# The Past

Integrity must be real,
with wishes to be admired.
Only with words and
actions can it convince one
it's genuine. A person can lead,
but must respond
to the values
of the masses.
That is where
motivation sits.
Pull up a seat
speak to all men
since they
are all equal.
Tell the stories to
others
of our founding fathers.

# Good vs Evil

Some things which we
think about
see as everyday
occurrences
may not come from nature.
ideas or concepts can be created
by man himself.
It's easy to think of the beauty
complexities of nature.
more difficult to reconcile
the idea of good and evil.
Are they created by a God
or ideas created in the mind of man?
Reference for man seems to exist
only in comparison.
Good and evil exist only in relation
to each other. All
things in nature must exist
in relation
to each other or good and evil was
created by a God.

# Remember

Wisdom once told us that
women had no sexual feelings,
their goal was pro-creation.
Doctors once found women who
enjoyed sex
declared as diseased.
They were forced to give up
any part of self,
to never grow up.
To be childlike forever.
How can one
grow up if they surrender
independence?
Women could not own
property and the belief - that
would make them free
of corruptions.

# Changes

The days of the great experiment
led to artistic changes.
Men can produce more goods
faster each day.
What is the cost of the quality?
The masses in time become content
with imperfect commodities.
In days long gone
before the ships came
to this land,
workmen did all they could
and stopped because
their art was complete.
It could not possibly
become any more beautiful.

# 50/50

A true leader of men needs
to be a risk taker
a person who doesn't need reinforcement
their deeds
because faith
and confidence is all
that is required.
One must understand
the reality of all
situations
and communicate the plan
confront it.
Criticism is always coming
unwarranted.
every person who loves you
there
is another who hates you.

# LSD # 2

They contaminated the land
and brought forth the prophet.
Coming from New York they
offend the other groups
the plural marriages.
Forced out they begin
a journey to the mid-west
several stops in several states
the prophet is imprisoned
then murdered.
This created
the grand exodus
by a new leader.
Now outside the U.S. territory
they flourished and transformed
a desert into its own world.

# Rich vs Poor

If you have something to do,
it matters not how you are clothed.
Only those who claim
to possess something
need to dress right.
A ripped jacket
shoes with holes
are just fine
when speaking to God.
He requires not a new suit
he will chastise
those who
those who spend time with conceit.
The true rich man
is he who can get an answer
from God no matter
what clothes he wears.

# WW III

It's only a brochure
maybe twelve thousand words.
the knowledge is simple,
class struggles are what keeps
a society in existence.
People dying over diamonds?
Wars fought for oil and pride?
It's a religion for some
excepted creed
for which one word has become sacred.
Millions are devoted to its principles
just as Christians are to the bible
With every terrorist act
we get closer to a war
ideology instead of a nuclear one.

# School

Children learn everyday about
a past leader of the United States.
Yet the names of Michael and
Raphael cannot be spoken.
Not as a simple theory.

Michael, leader of an army
carried into battle the mighty
sword in defiance of Gods enemies.
It was he who told Adam of
the history of mankind.

Raphael in his modest spirit tells
Adam and Eve of the raging battle,
Satan's plot to corrupt them.
Angels can lead nations as
well as men like George Washington.

# Free

A time ago man was
more concerned with equality
than with freedom.
Men feel free
when they are equal.
When no man has power
over another.
The ideal state
may be the only way
to possess this quality.
All men may be equal
but one must be the ruler.
It is he who dispenses agents
power among the supposed equal men.

# Nixon and an 8-Year-Old Boy

As a boy
I first heard of wiretapping.
It was done by the president
in order to obtain information
on his own citizens.
The paranoia made him
believe the other party
was at war with him,
America as well.
He tried to disrupt
like a coward he quit
leaving Americans humiliated,
an eight-year-old boy
afraid for the future.

# Apart

Feelings are most times
turned towards oneself. Man
wants to attach everything around
to themselves. To be an individual
is part of the nature God has
blessed all with. Each member of
every tribe needs at some point
to separate themselves from the
others.  Just as eventually each child
will draw apart from their parents.
Each needs to find others like them
to form bonds with. They can then
leave society to do as it will. Unless
it begins to interfere with the
groups collective thoughts.

# Associations

Political associates are simply
powerful people
who all wish to rule.
They recognize the sovereignty of
other associations
but will fight for their ideas
in all types of occasions.
By leading they direct
the communities
divert their attention
to the pursuit of that
which will
which will serve them as wealth.
If all groups are seeking the same
there will be tranquility
no revolution.
Then there will be no change.

# Beans

The problem we have today is
our president doesn't read much.
If he spent more time with
books, he would realize that the best
governments let the people live their
own lives. Politicians stay out of its
citizens day-to-day lives. They don't
tape the phones or check the email.
We the people does not give the president
this power. Government by nature
cannot rule on this basis of justice.
It rules by who is the strongest without
conscience. It's hard to follow a
leader when you can't tell one what
he stands.

# The Classes

The struggle starts at birth,
one by one they attack
against the instruments.
They will destroy the imports
and set fire to the buildings.
By force they will take
back their status in this
our world. They will unite the masses
and obtain political means. A
competition will develop forcing
the economy to fluctuate. Characteristics
soon begin to develop, a collision
between the classes will soon begin.

# They # 2

The Arawak relied on oral
traditions. They possessed not a
written word. They cultivated crops,
fished in the tropical sun
flourished without the calendar.
Then came the Spanish
the killers of
many societies and kings.
The scantily clad people
interacted with nature
and the spirits knew
of the sun, heavens, and earth.
They are now extinct
blood spilled
the ecological balance
of the earth
has been changed forever.

# The Disease

Some people dreamed of
a thousand-year reign, while
others were content with a
thousand days. Within this short
time it was assumed that the
disease was losing its strength.
That the United States could
by force stop the threat. A threat
of nuclear war may have only
slowed the spread. Without asking
those who put him upon the throne,
he put the children at risk. Then
the circle of advisors cost Americans
the lives of fifty thousand men.
The country was really no safer,
and the president was no less dead.

# Judgment Day

Sin the daughter of Satan
gives birth to Satan's son
then calls him death. He then
becomes the lover of his mother.
He is the discoverer of that
which causes men fear.

Together, mother and son, lovers
join to build the highway from
the gates of hell. Sin is the
gatekeeper and death possess the
dart, the killer of men.

Both will be defeated, as well as Satan
when judgment day begins with
the earth creature. Sides will be
chosen and many will die.

# Just Is

History has taught several
truths. One being that this
world is guided by a God. Great
things will soon be accomplished

by the meek. Suffering for truth
and a good death is the real
reason we are all here. We all
walk in a presence of a merciful life.

# Virtue

We never speak of virtue,
Even as we know of its usefulness.
We prove its existence every day,
by sacrificing for our fellow man.
Not because it is for the befallen,
but for what it imposes upon us.
Every person follows their own
Interests and in every person are
embedded the idea of virtue.
Montaigne followed the straight road,
only because of life's experiences,
not because it was the straightest.
This can be seen not only in
the poor, but the rich as well.

# Conversion

Native Americans are not Indians
but simply displaced believers
of the universe who never owned
any land. For they were the land.
Decimated by the diseases and the
Desire to destroy the heathens. The
cultures are gone. Christians claimed
to be the patrons of the spiritual
community. Sanctioned by the church
everyone should be converted
or put to death.

# Intellect

No revolution means there will
be no shake up of belief. One
needs to stand up to authority.
We need to release man and let
them doubt their ideas. It's in
mankind's interest
it's the doubt which transforms itself
into a togetherness. It brings them together,
that is what a new idea does.
All men will boast of thought
but few will ever act on it.
They need others to help them
fulfill their dreams.

# Settle

Mankind by birth wants
a fixed concept of God.
He needs to know the duties
Of his Lord and creator. By
this they can understand
their fellow man. If they did not know
what they have done
or what they can do. They would
abandon all means of action.
Giving way to total disorder.
It is too early in man's evolutionary stage
for him to settle on his own thoughts.

# Satan # 16

Evil by nature can be attractive
to man and God knows that.
Satan who was once a leader
In heaven still holds some of the
same virtues. Yet most of what
he speaks is lies. God created him
to sit at his side, but he chose
to revolt and wanted his own
place to reign. He took with him his
free will, but can only do what
God allows. He exists to give
validity to the light.

# Obligations

Religion can maintain
authority over man
in a democracy. If it
is only confined
to the spirit
it will have no place in commerce.
Its true value will be what it instills
and the external results
that come with it.
Religion imposes obligations on men
who fear the ideas
he doesn't understand.
All men are different
not all can have the same happiness
the creator gives all
the same conditions.

# Corrupt

On the throne of pandemonium
the debate has begun among
the devils. To ponder how to attack
mankind with open warfare or
by deception. Moloch and Beelzebub agree,
man must be attacked head on. The
other option was to seduce God's
creation, then take their revenge.
A volunteer is needed and Satan
himself wants the task. With shouts
of encouragement he is on his way
to corrupt man forever.

# World without Beasts

We are of course superior to all
other beasts. Our souls seek out
the material benefits for which God's
instincts have given us. We can rise against
issues of the soul. But, other beasts have
no notion. This is why
slavery seemed to exist for so long.
Until men realized the black man's soul
renders it capable of success.
They were not content
with just their freedom.
They need the soul to be strong
and content and live
for obtaining material objects.

# Politics

Important men know the value
and political importance of
Catholics, Negroes, and the Jews.
Some have appointed many to
posts within the government.
Not for their ability, but only
for the selfishness. The idea could
benefit the state. A new outlook
and social ideas come with the
numbers. A leadership role in politics
will then follow.

# Objects

A country unhappy with
religion and democracy, understood
how the two must coexist.
The philosophers or power seat sitters
should strive always to place the
objects of the crowds ahead of
their own means. Man seeks prosperity
the same in all countries. It's the
pure selfishness they must resist. The
temptation will always be right
in front of them.

# Mr. President

How a mining engineer
became president. It was his
business interests. A millionaire
with skills in international affairs,
often called by friends "Mr. Secretary."
His power of persuasion forced cooperation
resulting in a world dominated by corporations.
They split up the spoils and methodically
set prices to control the business cycle.
Factories were built my men
some feel they deserved the worship
of the
working class.

# Tree of Life

Work has no hereditary tree.
It's in every man, woman, and child.
Labor is what the country is based
on and lives have it in their mind.
It is the only truly honest thought
which we can concur. We have no
prejudice against it. No history or
generations who declare it evil. It
cannot be disputed as morally wrong
even the rich man feels compelled to
do something. It starts out sometimes
as public service.

# What do they Deserve?

Christianity tells of how we
should prefer others needs to
our own. This way the gain is an
upper hand on those who stand in line
for eternal life.
It's hard to believe
that the zealots work harder for
other people. Some speak openly of
the rewards and blessings they will
receive as it comes time to rest. Their
gift is to declare love for God. Do
they deceive themselves or do they
deserve great respect?

## Soma

You awake one day in
the detention center, not
thinking too clearly
it hits you.
Where is my everyday pill?
The reason I work, the
reason I get up. It's why
we have kids. The more kids
you have, the more workers
they get. In return the more
pills you get. Where are my kids?
They have my pills.